Bus Drivers

Julie Murray

Abdo Kids Junior
is an Imprint of Abdo Kids
abdopublishing.com

Abdo

MY COMMUNITY: JOBS

Kids

abdopublishing.com

Published by Abdo Kids, a division of ABDO, P.O. Box 398166, Minneapolis, Minnesota 55439.
Copyright © 2019 by Abdo Consulting Group, Inc. International copyrights reserved in all countries.
No part of this book may be reproduced in any form without written permission from the publisher.
Abdo Kids Junior™ is a trademark and logo of Abdo Kids.

Printed in the United States of America, North Mankato, Minnesota.

052018

092018

THIS BOOK CONTAINS
RECYCLED MATERIALS

Photo Credits: iStock, Shutterstock

Production Contributors: Teddy Borth, Jennie Forsberg, Grace Hansen

Design Contributors: Christina Doffing, Candice Keimig, Dorothy Toth

Library of Congress Control Number: 2017960550

Publisher's Cataloging-in-Publication Data

Names: Murray, Julie, author.

Title: Bus drivers / by Julie Murray.

Description: Minneapolis, Minnesota : Abdo Kids, 2019. | Series: My community: Jobs |
    Includes glossary, index and online resources (page 24).

Identifiers: ISBN 9781532107863 (lib.bdg.) | ISBN 9781532108846 (ebook) |
    ISBN 9781532109331 (Read-to-me ebook)

Subjects: LCSH: Bus Drivers--Juvenile literature. | Public transportation--Juvenile literature. |
    Occupations--Careers--Jobs--Juvenile literature. | Community life--Juvenile literature.

Classification: DDC 388.322--dc23

Table of Contents

Bus Drivers

Kevin gets on the bus. Who does he see? The bus driver!

Drivers follow a route.

They need to be on time.

They stop at bus stops.

Josh gets on the bus.

Mara sits in her seat.

She follows the rules.

The driver makes sure everyone is safe.

13

Sara turns on the flashers.

She puts the stop sign out.

Cars must stop.

Pat drives a city bus.

Cities can be busy. Driving a big bus is not easy!

Jae drives a school bus. The kids are on time for school!

A Bus Driver's Tools

bus

map of route

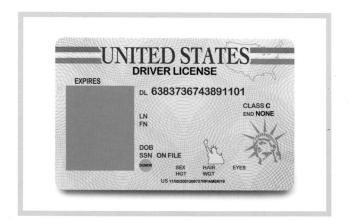

special class license

two-way radio

Glossary

flashers
lights on a bus that tell other drivers to yield or stop.

route
a road of travel from one place to the next that a bus follows every day.

Index

Abdo Kids ONLINE

FREE! ONLINE MULTIMEDIA RESOURCES

Visit **abdokids.com** and use this code to access crafts, games, videos, and more!

Abdo Kids Code:
MBK7863